Life Is
Not
All About
Work

Published by Career Choice Press

For more information or to request permission to quote from this book, contact the author by e-mail at careerchoiceblog@gmail.com or visit http://www.careerchoiceonline.com/

Cover image: Khakimullin Aleksandr/Shutterstock

First Printing: October 29, 2017

Printed in the United States of America

ISBN: 978-0-9995532-0-6

Acknowledgements

We are all blessed and born with our select personal gifts. In reminiscence, I possess many an unfinished draft. Perseverance however has paid off, and I must begin by thanking the almighty God for allowing me to finish this project.

The writing of Life Is Not All About Work has become a noteworthy journey. I am grateful to Fred Chandler whose wisdom and experience in Workforce Development was used to reassure me of the substantive nature in this specialized compilation of verse and poetry.

I must recognize my longtime friend Alicia Gage who, from across the Atlantic dedicated her time and talent as an Editor... thank you Alicia.

Carole Kupelian has read and critiqued every significant paper I have written in the last 20 years. Her expertise and commitment to my success is unfathomable... thanks again Carole.

Thanks to Gequanne Cabey for following me around and taking photographs until we found one that the team could live with.

But, it was Julie 'Jules' Abramson whose gifts as a Graphic Designer brought it all together. Thanks Julie for your patience, the thought provoking questions and for tapping your network for the benefit of this project.

I must also express my appreciation to my wife Wivinia, our extended family and everyone who has provided encouragement, moral support and inspiration that made the writing of this book possible.

Life Is Not All About Work

Contents

Index of Titles

Foreword

his compilation of verse, poetry, limericks and self-assessments are intended to help individuals focus on who they are... and challenge each person to keep themselves at the top center of their lives.

Presenting the details in this format is purposed to lighten the traditionally stressful subject of career planning and decision making, which for many job seekers can be a daunting process. It is the author's hope that as you read the contents of each line you may also absorb the intended message.

Life is not all about work. For those of us with lesser means however, work often becomes our life...A HORRID WAY TO LIVE!

Thus, as working professionals, time must be invested in not only our immediate needs, but in the future and lifestyle we most desire. This may require moving away from the familiar in order to acquaint 'one's self' with 'what else', 'what's next' and, 'what's the worst that can happen if I...'? The depth of these key questions are often overlooked by job seekers and career practitioners alike.

This composition is designed to energize your next move. In the midst of reading and analyzing each line, you are also encouraged to recognize the humor. Do not pass up a moment to laugh, smirk or even kick yourself... the edutainment is deliberate. You may also be aware that a moment of laughter can reduce your stress levels. Always keep in mind it is much easier to think, plan, as well as make career and life changing decisions when the head and mind are clear and free from life's clutter.

Life Is Not All About Work

CHAPTER 1

A Place of Service

Overview

It is not what you say, but how it is said.
It is not the quality and certainly not the quantity,
but the attitude with which services are delivered.
Do you listen with an open mind, advise with caring
and politeness, educate, train and motivate others
with humility and respect? These are the goals of
this chapter.

Whether or not you are being adequately compensated,
do you enjoy the time spent at work? And, if you are
being made to feel less than, perhaps it is time to seek
opportunities elsewhere in order to avoid causing
discomfort to others as well as preserve your own
peace of mind. Read on...

Empowerment

*Fear and tear may enter here
But only the empowered will leave.*

My Workspace

Within my workspace
I am in charge
Every action, every decision
Gets the best I can give

Within my workspace
I must be self-paced
Every move is deliberate
Every outcome correct

Within my workspace
Everyone is welcomed
To share a bright moment
A laugh that's sincere

Within my workspace
There's always time for fun
That's the way I know works best
To get assigned chores done.

Choose Productivity

I will have a productive day
Nothing, no one will upset my sway
I'll choose a rhythm that keeps me movin'
Then energy and drive will tug me in.

Call me by my name

Label me as being respectful
Label me as being humble
Label me as being knowledgeable
Label me being honest
Label me as being kind
Label me as being caring
Label me as being committed
Label me as being helpful
Or just call me by my name

Refer to me as confident
Refer to me as competent
Refer to me as resilient
Refer to me as supportive
Refer to me as witty
Refer to me as intelligent
Refer to me as kind
Refer to me as persistent
Refer to me as organized
Refer to me as open-minded
Refer to me as someone with a positive outlook
Or simply refer to me by my name.

Fun At Work

The workplace must be fun
For all who enter in
Some joys of work come from jobs well done
But more from the mem'ries lasting...

Work's Destructive Side

When at work, be fully committed
so that upon leaving
you can leave it all behind.
Taking work home whether mentally or physically
is a destroyer of family life
it disrupts one's life balance
is a primary ingredient in burnout and,
only the employer benefits.

Give us a break!

Not so long ago, the place to catch up with the office
gossip was at the water cooler.
Employers pledged to put a stop to this;
So, they got rid of the water cooler.
This became a reason for gossip!
Now employees miss the water but,
Losing the water cooler hurts more.
They have lost that place
To relax for a moment, to unwind -
Employees are now stuck at their desks
Losing poise, changing in size, dying from chairs
Nowhere to go to discuss politics, office politics -
Get a momentary break from the grind…
They feel constantly scrutinized
No get-away to clear and refresh their minds:
Another stressor,
Lost motivation,
Less productivity,
Time used to plan their next move.
And before long!
A once secure work environment
Has become a costly revolving door
And everyone loses.

No Clue

Aren't you perturbed when a long time co-worker approaches and starts telling you that Ms. or Mr. ____ died and you have no clue who they are talking about?

How do you respond?

Justly Rewarded

We have lots of parties at the office
It is a very relaxed environment
Celebrations are the norm
But we remain on task too
The epitome of multitasking
So we work hard
Weekly turning over millions
Consistently exceeding expectations
And are handsomely rewarded
Because management notices.

A Game of Numbers

It's been said over and over again that
the numbers don't lie.
You may also have heard sayings like
"united we stand…" and
"in unity there is strength" among others.
If you believe in numbers but doubted
the other sayings above, look at the facts below:

Together = 98
Separate = 79

Collective = 106
Individual = 105

Group = 77
Alone = 49

The next time you are asked to join the team,
the union, participate in a group effort,
or serve on a committee, remember,
the numbers don't lie and
there is strength in unity.
And, while we are doing the numbers,
Attitude = 100
Gratitude = 106
Show gratitude to the person who
encouraged you to get involved.

The Working Class Echoes

I have to work
I want to work
What am I going to do if I don't work?
I love what I do
I love the people that I work with, we are friends
I love all my customers
I have bills to pay
I can't afford to retire
They will carry me out in a box.

Understanding Our World

*To fully understand our world,
one must first appreciate
and accept its many colors.*

Dead End

Everyday is different!
Today there was guest drama
Yesterday new gadgets were delivered
And tomorrow there is no telling
with a staff that is ever dwindling
No room for growth,
Everyone's on the move
Such a workplace is not one to love.

The Choice

Academic homework assigned in class
is rewarding to the student;

CHOICE!

Taking home work assignments
from your job is rewarding to the employer.

E-mail Communication

E-mail may be a great resource for speedy
Communication, but, it has also become
the most burdensome means of sharing
information in the workplace.
Here are a few things 'bosses' need to consider
before sending an e-mail:
It limits communication and interaction between
management and staff;
But that might be the goal!

It destroys moral in the work environment;
That might be goal number two!

Various studies have revealed that E-mail
eats up over 40 percent of the staff's day.
Thus, if the motive is to highlight how badly an
employee manages their time or to expose
their weak grammatical abilities…
What better way to do it than with an e-mail?
Goal number three perhaps!

First log-on, (Mmmm…What is my password?)
Then login, open, read, interpret and now,
more time is lost having to write the response.
Assignments are delayed, then of course,
performance standards drop because
deadlines are not being met…
Is setting staff up to fail goal number four?

The truth is - whether e-mail is being employed as a tool of oppression or not, the topic being debated is seldom ever resolved via this medium. Time would be much more effectively utilized doing the job that the e-mail tries to address. Experience has shown that the details stated in an e-mail could be resolved in a 30 second telephone or face to face conversation.

So what is the point of e-mail exchanges with colleagues who are across or down the hall if not to document and track. Could it be that true feelings and communication impotence are hidden behind this technological mask? Since organizations know the limitations of e-mail in workplace communication, isn't it time to get back to the business of facing your colleagues?
IT IS TIME FOR MANAGERS TO STOP WASTING THEIRS AND EMPLOYEES' TIME!
I just raised my voice didn't I? So-o-o-r-r-ry!

But, wait, before moving on...
I almost forgot to **"REPLY ALL"....**
That would be a really bad miss.... Oops!
Thank God I caught it before hitting **SEND.**

Please share!

Only Enthusiasm

I arrived at my workplace today
Filled with enthusiasm, energy and sway
So when old grouch stepped in my way
In simple language I smiled and said
Not today grouchy, not today.

Cut The Noise

A lot more would be accomplished if there were less noise, distractions and diversions!

Routine

When your routine becomes routine, perhaps it is time to change your routine to avoid boredom, frustration and burnout.

Share Inspiration

Words can hurt, words can heal
Words can impact how anyone feels
Choose positive language
Stimulate positive thinking
Let everyone you meet leave with something inspiring

Pictures will do if graphic images you prefer
Provoke the mind with passive signs
Evoke clean thoughts from –
That heavy heart, stuck mind, or curious soul
Allow silence as inspiration takes hold

Conversation will flow when barriers come down
No guessing where common ground will be found
A cause to pause, a moment for reflection
If actions are sincere, the message will be clear
From entrance to boardroom, your goal is to inspire.

A Place to Serve

Efficient service is all I offer
Each day to whomever I serve
From start to finish
Respect and my best is given
Without fail to colleagues and clients

Life happens here that I can say
Some call it a workplace
It's where I play
And at days end, I plan again
Ways to enhance my service for others gain.

Limericks – 1

Smile

Work efficiently to complete each task
Deliver with grace all the boss asks
Get everything done
With timely completion
And share the smile that's not a mask.

Limericks – 2

No Gratitude

Everyone sought from start until closing
A coworker of mine that knew everything
He received little thanks
Even less for the bank
And without notice left them all wanting.

Limericks – 3

Teamwork

Teamwork of itself is a task
Says every team member you ask
Together we're fun
And if there is sun
Nothing gets done for in it we bask.

Limericks – 4

Christmas Party

The staff party last Christmas was grand
Music blasted all night from the band
The music was good
And so was the food
Until a drunk colleague asked for my hand.

Limericks – 5

Supervisor From Hell

There was a supervisor from hell
Who taunted the workplace with a bell
It rang a naughty chime
That really didn't rhyme
T'was a relief that it broke when it fell.

Limericks – 6

Without A Clue

There was a pretty clueless supervisor
Always sought help from a junior worker
They gave him no respect
And one you'll never suspect
Said, be advised, I'm not your broker.

CHAPTER 2

Nurturing the Entire Me

Overview

All too often, jobseekers accept an offer for employment only to become so caught up in their tasks, the income and their professional selves that they forget who they are as individuals – human beings with a personal life to live and other responsibilities to manage.

This chapter urges you to keep yourself, your family and friends in focus. Given the fickle nature of our current job market, employees need to remember that everything is only for a time. Thus, keep yourself, your value, your values and your priorities at the forefront of your life.

Prayer and Positive Energy

I will begin each day with a prayer
Or a positive thought that is well meaning
Coming straight from my heart
To all I serve and in all I do
This energy flows from God through me to you

Share Motivation

I shared a motivating word today
With someone I barely knew
Thank you, Thank you, repeatedly I heard
Genuinely smiling as he walked away

Perhaps an idea was spawned
Perhaps a seed was sown
Perhaps reinforcement only was sought
Perhaps clarity to a stuck mind was brought

That motivating word I shared
May that life forever impact
And as time passes passed on to others
A happy smiles virus from which no one is spared.

Hope

Hang a poster on the wall
Inspiring words for those who call
Pictures will do if you prefer
Messages of hope must be loud and clear.

My Integrity

Numbers do not define
Contributions made on this spot
My integrity they don't impact
For those I serve and in all I do
To me I remain true.

Pleasant Thoughts

I thought of you today
As I got on my way
Pleasant thoughts made me smile
Warmed my heart, cleared my mind
Made my journey worthwhile
And stayed with me all day.

Grateful Heart

I will fill my day with joy and sway
Neither distractors nor detractors
Will get in my way
And at days end I will smile
And with a grateful heart I'll say
Thank you God, for another productive day.

Drive

I rise at the crack of dawn each day
For duty calls and I must obey
For the love of family
and the privileged life I lead
To the institution I must drive
If I am to thrive.

I rise at the crack of dawn each day
And leave midst rain, sleet, sunshine or snow
My resting family sees me not
Nor do they know my call
They'll never know what drives me on
And won't before I fall.

I rise at the crack of dawn each day
And never leave before I pray
For wisdom and safe travels
For family, colleagues, friends and all
For humility, patience and ability to serve
Each client with the respect that they deserve

I rise at the crack of dawn each day
And with breakfast and lunch I drive away
Eating on the road, between key strokes at the desk
I swallow food and carry on with the task
For when day ends and the jobs are complete
Dinner with family is my most welcome treat.

The Outcome

An enjoyable journey
may make the destination more rewarding.

Appreciation

A friend reached out to me
I am heavily overwhelmed said he
After pausing a moment I replied hastily
The air is fresh and clean, why not step outside?
Here's an honest smile and
A motivating word or two
It's all I can offer, all I can give
In appreciation for all that you do.

Twice a Loser

Rushing on your way to work and rushing to get home from work makes the traveler a loser twice in one day.

So, you arrive:
Tired, flustered, anxious, stressed
Momentarily you're useless at best
To family or situation
Your state of mind is a big mess
Now more time is spent
waiting to recover, to unwind
From the risks,
The hassle of the hustle and bustle!
Why not sit back?
Soak up the scenery, enjoy the journey
Pity those demonstrating idiotic behaviors.
Why drive in frenzy?
Pace yourself! Be amused by the foolery
Get to your destination relaxed,
refreshed and ready for duty.

Give Thanks

Show appreciation
For all that others do
Be it something simple
Be it great or something new.

'Tis the little things that count they say
But the big things matter too
Show appreciation every day
And even greater things will happen for you.

It may not be what you expect
Returns may not come right away
When! is the answer you can't predict
But that's not what 'thank you' should say.

With sincerity express gratitude
As often as you can
While wondering or wandering
Ponder a reason to give thanks.

Show appreciation
For every person that you meet
For stuck-ups who don't seem to see
And those who keep our surroundings clean.

For clothing, for food and shelter
The work you and others do
And when the journey is over
Show appreciation for safe travels too.

Show appreciation
Show gratitude for the talent you own
For sleeping, waking and being blessed
Give to those with no place to rest.

Humility will strengthen your core
Be grateful to those who came before
And with those who always stand by you
Pray for those destined to follow.

Gratitude you must express
For the lifestyle that you possess
For the wrongs that impeded your way
And knowledge that cleared the grey.

Show appreciation
For family and loved ones near
And for all those you've not yet met
Let them know from your heart you care.

Thankfulness we must express
For the ever changing seasons
Dry, wet, sunny, windy or freezing
And the difference each change brings.

Show appreciation
From dawn to dusk each day
Cherish energy continuously rising
Allow positive forces to spread.

Let's all be forever grateful
For the privilege to serve
Or else how could we justify
Our human purpose here on earth?

Contributions

People come and go each day
Lifetimes o'er and o'er
Whatever they take or contribute
In one way or the other
It's always an attribute.

Health Matters

Whether it is paid up front
Or after the damage is done
Health matters!
Choosing wisely now
You may hear voices go wow
As you gracefully stroll along the sidewalk
To the eatery that best supports
Your diet and palate
Confidently enter your next place of business
Or enter the gym to relax and relieve stress
Whether one does all of the above or neither
Remember, healthy habits matter!

Lost In Ignorance

Ears constantly plugged
A ploy designed to deafen
Destabilize and control the mind
Eyes glued, staring at a screen
Print so small, lighting harmful to the eyes,
Always glaring;
In the short term blinding
Long term vision deprived
Hands occupied
Palms hug radiation-spreading gadget
Elbows bent
Locked in position toward forward leaning head
Ten pound weight straining the frail neck
Taking away the scenery
The power of observation
Peeling away the senses
Absent now is commonsense
Life becomes lying around
Dispossessed of talent acquisition
Limited advanced speech and language application
The future of human kind
Rendered deaf, crippled and blind
Ignorance forever alive now thrives.

Happy Thoughts

Bring happy thoughts to work each day
Share them with everyone in your way
And at the hour when day's end comes
Take them with you as you leave for home.

Waste

Dying to get to work and dying to get home from work is a waste and makes no difference.

My Health is My Business

Being healthy, wealthy and wise are age old goals.
Spend enough time reflecting on these simple
words and you will soon realize they are hugely
co-dependent. A wise person who values life will do
all that it takes to manage their lifestyle in order to
remain healthy. This individual knows that having a
healthy body and mind are the necessary ingredients
for not only longevity, but are the driving force
behind the fulfillment of our goals and dreams…
These may include a desire to achieve financial
wealth. In the 21st century our livelihood is the push
of a button away. Dietary options are at an all-time
high, yet medical doctors continue to invest precious
time in advising and caring for individuals whose
choices have led them to obesity and related
maladies. Employers and government agencies
dread this virus. Education has failed to slow its
spread. Meanwhile, access to medical technology
and cheap background checks make it easy for
potential employers to examine the whole package
before setting eyes on the person. Thus, we are at
a point in history when anything but good health
can restrict our professional growth and ultimately
become a barrier to success and wealth. Today, the
rising cost of living is occurring simultaneously with
a rapid and steady decline in income levels.

This should prompt us to ponder the impact of, and relationship between, good health and wealth. Knowing that obesity is an unhealthy option, the wise are conditioning for healthy and wealthy lifestyles using motivational statements like the age old saying: "I want nothing about me fat except my wallet." *(Inspired by Bruce DeLauder 3/22/2017)*

Whenever your personal health is called into question, become selfish.

Take action!

Laugh

A pause to think about your daily task
Will show that there's humor in everything we do.
What is one thing that happened at work today
about which you can laugh?

Stop Stressing

Anything that negatively impacts your stress level or is a cause for worry negatively affects your work-life balance.

In the Unfamiliar

The GPS was chosen
Technological guide venturing an unfamiliar pathway
Destination certain
Narrow, winding roadway unknown
Yet with perseverance through uncertainty
The way is found
Navigating through a vista of serenity
Bypassing greenery fronted by blooming flora
Designed to enhance the grandeur
of overpriced real estate…
Few could truly afford.
And, as it snakes around,
Each bend opens up a new sight
Unveiling a scene more picturesque
than the segment before.
But suddenly,
The smooth black-topped roadway ends
Circling back to columns of box shaped high rises
Glory descends once again into a bustling highway
Leaving a lasting memory
Fellow commuters may someday capture.
Still, the journey lives on…
With a longing for tomorrow's dawn, when,
Driven by a desire for adventure
GPS is replaced by landmarks of glamour
And this moment of ecstasy will return.

Rush Hour

Rush hour was not intended for people commuting to and from work in a hurry.

Risk Rewarded

Today I skipped the jammed highway
And tranquility I found
Along a lesser used bi-way
Where fallen leaves carpet the ground.

Today I skipped the jammed highway
For a narrow winding path
At the start admittedly daunting
Such evergreen beauty few commuters have seen.

Today I skipped the jammed highway
And experienced a calming feel
My spiritual side for so long shelved
In this moment it-self unveiled.

Today I skipped the jammed highway
To taste nature's earthy scents
Smiled at the artwork of sun spots
Found peace of mind, jammed highway never again!

State of Mind

I will always lead with an open mind
And a positive attitude
I will utilize resources I find
That keep me in the mood.

Aspiration

Today my thoughts are aiming high
Wandering into that corner office in the sky
And though that space is not yet mine
To view from this humble workplace now is fine.

Say Thank You

Welcome compliments with grace and humility.
They are the everlasting benefits
of your contributions to humanity.

Loyalty

True friends will go the extra mile for each other
Committed employees will go above and beyond
for their employers,
Soldiers will die for their comrades,
Parents will give life and limb to protect their
children...

However, true friends, committed employees,
soldiers and parents will often go only so far and no
further in search of rewards themselves.

**Loyalty and commitment are among the
most common of human values.**

The Price of Success

Someone made a sacrifice
Someone at onetime paid a price
For real success to be achieved
This approach has been proven indeed.

Limerick—7

Talent Killer

Detangle yourself from the media
Mostly noise to distract and deceive ya
No room to build on ideas
Or overcome your fears.
Social media is one talent killah.

CHAPTER 3

When Bosses
Are In Charge...

Overview

The goal of the next few pages is to shed light on workplace
behaviors, and particularly the way in which 'At Will' has
dehumanized and desensitized businesses, corporations and
even government-run agencies. If your experience is different,
PLEASE! Cherish each and every moment.
Nevertheless, read on...

Undying Support

Isn't it somewhat amusing that all of the 'leaders'
in a declining organization hold similar points of
view and tend to support each other's line of
thinking on a broad range of topics?

Questions Anyone?

One of the most frustrating issues for employees are bosses who ask "Do you have any questions?" during or towards the end of a 'here's what you will do' or 'here's how the process is going to work' meeting.

If no one responds, some will pretend to be concerned, others will act surprised and still others will be relieved.

On the other hand, if you want to reverse the frustration, asking a question about anything related to the process just outlined may set you up for the stare and perhaps a vague often off topic diversion.
Beware!

Shocking Relief

You're fired.
What!
You're fired.
Heard a second time was cause for a pause
This command was not serious, how could it be?
Then it registered, leaving an awkward silence
Standing face to face midst the noise of surprised breathing
A million thoughts roamed through my brain
Yet I remained in place, transfixed
For all I'd done, the years I'd spent
My commitment!
Giving up life's events with family and friends
In a moment's notice, 'twas all taken
So, in shock I stood in place, frozen
The heat of anger lighting up my face
Bastard! I thought, okay! I muttered
As I turned and walked away
Feeling the angry emotions flowing down my cheeks -
I let them run.
Walking toward my former office
The anger quickly passed
It's going to be okay was the intervening thought
And a slouch in ten paces
Evolved into squared shoulders
Integrity held my head upright
Confidence returned.
As I entered what for years was my earning space
Productivity, meetings, laughter, discussions,
disagreements — a feeling of loss overwhelmed me,

Recognizing that it took only three words to swipe it all away was painful.

You're fired!
In that moment, eons of memories were replaced by nothing.
To be honest, it had been sometime coming
And I'd begun preparing.
Still it was hard to swallow...
You're fired!
Words that rocked my very core...
Temporarily blank, I had no answer.
Looking at the desk, there was nothing left.
Sensing instability, proactive me had moved it all before...
except for my little lunch kit.
This thought triggered a smile and in that bittersweet
moment, I dried my eyes...
No more tears!
"Stop crying silly" I muttered,
Now feeling a strong sense of pride
This place had given me life,
I'd accomplished a lot.
Butter for my bread, a place to lay my head,
And, college tuition now fully paid.
For a while this encumbrance was my everything.
A thought that made this moment distinctive
You're fired!
Words I'd heard about but never before heard!
Quietly I chuckled as I found my car keys
And rid myself of theirs.
Feeling relieved, there was only the boss to see
As I sashayed through the door
My lunch kit, my keys, and me.

The Win-Win

In a meeting between Psychologists and Business Managers to discuss strategies for improving the mental health of employees by reducing work induced stress, the business managers stated: those that are stressed will come to your practice and we will hire new staff. It's a win-win!

Capitalism

To managers of businesses that hire
Nothing else seems to matter
But the almighty dollar
A practice that's spilling over
From buyers to sellers, contractors to laborers
Doctors to patients, hotels to patrons
And the list goes on and on
Without throwing away your value
And giving up your values
Employee, selfish you must be,
To keep a fair share
Of the dollar that you earned.
For when the month ends
Its share capitalism demands
And every bill you owe must be paid.

Common Cents

In the process of acquiring and
accumulating $$$, keep some common cents.

Communication Killer

E-mail is the silent killer of communication in the workplace. Preserve the life of your company, work environment and business relationships: communicate verbally (face to face or via telephone) with the staff, your partners and coworkers.

Leadership Myth

Our world is filled with bosses
Called by different names
Manager, supervisor, team-lead, political leader
Common titles used to motivate and maim
Lumped together their jobs are much the same
They push followers through paces, creative or mundane.

Many serve really well and fair
Guided by rules, respect and rapport
They communicate knowledge sound and true
Demonstrating trustworthiness and tact
Will challenge status and battle for truth
These are leaders through and through.

There are those of less understanding
Trailing ages of subtle abuses
That stems from limited reading
And with experience severely lacking
Inspire crowds of weaklings
To exploit the mediocrity of floundering systems.

With attitudes worthy of amateurs
They are chronically insecure
Driven by vice and limited intellect
And given the best these leaders possess
Fear bolsters their immature ways
To strike down any upstart venturing into their space.

Amateur or immature, somehow it doesn't matter.
Fledglings hustle when they roar
Some qualified others won't be denied
They rule with oppressive force
And those who should be disqualified
Hold lofty roles attained from a nepotistic source.

What do I do? How does this get done?
Confusion spoils their faces
Erratic acts thrive, stupidity undisguised
Nowhere at work will they feel secure
But in leaderships highest office you'll see
A world bossed by immature amateurs.

A Tip For Novice Bosses

When your staff stops talking to you, be assured that they are talking about you. And, very rarely is the subject being discussed a positive attribute.

Let Me Be!

The voice of a veteran employee during the annual review meeting with a disrespectful novice supervisor:

I love working here...

Thoroughly enjoy the work I do

I possess excellent skills, have years of experience

I am efficient and get along well with others,

Even those who consistently demonstrate

unprofessional conduct;

I do not get caught up in office gossip but am aware

of activities and participate as time allows...

If this meeting is over,

May I return to doing the one thing I enjoy here!

Defining TEAM

TEAM - the entire group.

ME - each individual, their roles and contributions

MA - the leader: Respected, knowledgeable, impartial, the guiding force

TEA - break time – time to regroup and reassess Actions, achievements and prepare next steps.

MEAT - the core, the mission, the purpose, the Bottom-line, the reason the team was put together.

Once committed, this cohesive unit will remove barriers, overcome challenges, break new ground and fight off the naysayers.

_____ team will become the face of the organization it represents.

Limerick – 8

Followers

Followers they all really are
As 'leaders' these bosses don't care
Unskilled bureaucrats
Travelling like blind bats
They seem to run into walls everywhere.

Limericks – 9

The Meeting

There was a meeting long planned
To discuss how departments are manned
The meeting was bad
And another was had
Where it was told that our program was banned.

Limerick – 10

The Confession

Confession to future generations
Parents had no say in the decision
The destruction you find
Was put in place by unkind
Corporations and greedy politicians.

Limerick – 11

Unappreciated

There was an experienced worker
Who year after year worked without falter
Then one wintry day
He could not make his way
And they sacked the experienced old feller.

Limerick - 12

Teens At Work

Do work youngster put the gadget away
Said the overseer to teen charge everyday
You should learn this some time
Though you're well past your prime
O M G work is more fun when you play.

Limerick – 13

Rule Changers

In our world of capitalist rule
Dollar cravings turn men into fools
They have low tolerance
For anyone who doesn't
Play by their book of ever changing rules.

CHAPTER 4

Find Your
Best Fit Position...

Overview

The job search process in many industries has become increasingly daunting. Application requirements for the most menial of positions - including volunteer roles, are very often intimidating. Finding employment in the current employer-controlled marketplace requires even the best among outstanding applicants to endure three, four, sometimes five or more rounds of interviews.

Reinforcing this stressful elimination process is the discrimination from which no race, religion, political affiliation, age group, military service, ex-convict, ethnic group, family member, sexual orientation, disability, or gender, is spared. Explore some strategies that have been proven to enhance the successful jobseeker's marketability during this tough and enduring marathon. Read on...

Stage, Not Age

Avoid aging yourself! Focus instead on the current stage of your life and highlight the talent and expertise that you have to offer. The job search process is often slow... Be Patient!

Have A Plan

Plan your plan
Outline your plan
Implement your plan
Work to your plan
Give your plan time to work
When all of the above are done right
Your plan will work for you.

Present your best

A female jobseeker stood in line
Hoping to meet with an employer of mine
Her shoulders were bared
Spaghetti straps shared
With everyone standing behind
Quietly I asked her to join me for a word
Which to my request she agreed
We reviewed her attire
And with cheeks lit afire
She said sir I have nothing else to wear
A spontaneous proposal I made her
One she considered
And hastily darted
To find a friend with a blouse to lend
She returned moments later
Shoulders now fully covered
Wearing a smile of gratitude
Her meeting came quickly
And the employer she did see
For an interview no other would beat
She was instantly hired
For the position being offered
Her skills and appearance
Were ideal and the perfect fit.

Your Résumé

Just as your suitcase is always packed when living in a
disaster zone
So your résumé should always be ready and at hand;
There's no telling when the door to your current position
will close or from where the next call will come.

Interviewing Tips

Adapt an athlete's mindset
Research and prepare thoroughly
Stick to your game plan
Do not hold back information
Be cool and confident
Leave everything that is relevant
In the interview room.
Don't exert more energy than you need to.

Discrimination in Brief

Have you thought about the actual reason that it's been so difficult to find a really good paying position? Yes! And as painful as it is, I sometimes find it really funny and would just burst out laughing at the fallacy of this whole hiring business. It is not easy but unless one can see the humor that drives this ignorance, lunacy will set in. Don't you wonder why so many of the gifted and talented resort to clandestine operations, or reach a level of depression that forces them round the bend or cause them to go over into the deep end?
Listen…

"Sir: you have excellent qualifications and experience, but we do not think this position will be a good fit for you." Or

"Ma'am: we are looking for someone who specializes in the following technical areas, and we do not see those skills among your expertise." Continue to look at our website.

Here's another…

"Ms. _____, you are exceptionally qualified to fulfill the responsibilities of this position but your credentials have not been forwarded to the hiring manager. This position is reserved for someone with military experience, and I see that you are not a veteran."
The truth is, I am a veteran. Experience of any value or in any quantity is an obstacle for me. Also, I don't really know anyone who works for the company. The other big problem I face is the disability issue, and mine is the complexion of my heritage, and the accent that is a natural part of my culture.
So! With all the skills and experience that you possess, why not start your own business?
I am working on that.
Would you hire me? I know that I don't have all the education and skills, but we are friends and I am young, committed, willing to work hard and learn. You could even pay me a little less.
Of course! I would hire you because I like you.

A Jobseeker's Journey

To speed up or ease up is the choice!
This road through life with its many
Junctions and multiple intersections
Allowing for the demands of constant movement
Always hoping for smooth transitions
As mergers connect from every direction
Changing lanes is not an easy option;
Approaching each interchange
Is an agonizing decision
Speed up or ease up!
There-in lies the risk -
What are the pros?
How might one benefit?
To crash and burn at this juncture
Would at any rate be a grave disaster
Pace estimate must be ever accurate
Slower sometimes, or other times faster
There's never room to give way
As every counterpart's action says 'game on'
Course must at all cost, be on point
Of significance is effective management of time
New destination without notice comes into view

Nerves warn with its now familiar twitch -
Speed up, or slow down?
That nagging question!
But keep going is a must
Clear directive from the mind
As multiple roles are played out on reflex
Moment by moment monitoring the traffic
There-in lies the competition
That makes this challenging career pathway fun;
Still, this life is a serious game
The strong will survive
But the persistent will win!
Keep moving, no matter what, keep moving!
Tap every available resource -
Windscreen, rearview and side mirrors
Each contributes to the vision
Bringing differing perspectives to a mission
Designed to outlast every other contender
As the next opening lights up yonder
In this adventure, opportunity knows no waiting
Always moving, listening, learning
Weaving through curves, negotiating sharp turns,
Hastily adjusting tempo to sudden rises and falls
Working to maintain consistency of flow -

A well-oiled machine on the go!
 Career minded, profession centered
There's no going back on this track
Forward remains the only motion
Technology supported, intrinsically motivated
Communicating, observing, sharing
Believing this is my time, my time to strike
My time to build, my time to strive
My time to fulfill those pent up childhood dreams
I keep moving
Faster now than before
The only risk is losing my place
This won't happen lest I fall from grace
So onward I press!
Focused, now sensing an advantage
Another intersection emerges
Beyond which is success to conquer
There can be no easing up
No margin for error
Home trumps hope at this juncture
And asserting that I am the best on this run
I travel on.
(Inspired by Wivi Edgecombe 4/8/2017)

Three Seconds

You may not care about looks
And even less about how you are looked at
But in the moment of decision that lasting
impression may have been determined in the first
Three (3) seconds.

Relevance Sells

"Am I relevant?" I asked. I have the knowledge no doubt! Do I really possess the skills and maturity to function effectively in that environment? Will I even fit in? And suppose I don't! What if I am not liked or appreciated? Will they keep me?

I wonder if they would provide training in areas where I might not be so well versed! I highly doubt it, but I will ask...they just might. Yes, I will ask...that's what I will do. At the next interview, I will ask if they provide skills based training. What else should I have to be relevant?

I need to get along with other people - whether or not they look like me, I must be able to adapt, fit into the team and be on my game. I communicate extremely well in all three areas: listening, speaking and writing.

In the technology arena, in spite of the constant changes, I am as good as anyone and I use various social media forums. I know my industry well and I can fit into most organizations. I have to join a professional organization and get myself a mentor.

This new position is going to demand a lot of me. I need guidance and am open to new opportunities, paradigms, even have some ideas that I can share.
I can do this! "Am I relevant?"
YES!

Free Spirit

I don't know what I am good at
And don't care to for what that's worth
An open minded free spirited soul
Watch as I wander around the globe.

There must be something you can do
Some say you must do something
But looking at the lives of you and you
I love the life that lets me spread my wings.

Career Decision Making

Do you understand the job search Process?
There are a multiplicity of layers in the job search
process and, unlike an onion where for every layer that
comes off the next looks similar but is smaller, each
layer in the job search process tends to have its own
requirements and are often more complex and
demanding of the jobseeker. Following are some basic
steps that will help you with exceeding the employers'
expectations:

A. Research the company/organization

B. Know your industry...
1. Are the jobs
      a.) Seasonal
      b.) Contractual
      c.) Compensatory
      d.) Salaried

II. What are the trends?
      a.) What is the hiring process?
      b.) Is job hopping okay?
      c.) What key skills do you need?

III. Who are the movers and shakers?

IV. Are you involved in a professional association?

C. Examine your skills and interests and identify your preferred work environment. These aspects are often overlooked by many jobseekers. In our technology driven culture however, a little research might help jobseekers to realize that your HTML or Programming skills may be applicable in a social services or not for profit organization, similarly to those of an accountant who manages the bookkeeping and accounts for the same agency instead of an accounting firm. Knowing yourself, and your values could place you in your perfect work environment even if you are applying a different skill set.

What are your goals...which track are you on? Is this position a means to an end (Professional/Job hopping approach) or do you want to keep this position until retirement (Career focused)?

Do you have current job search skills and tools?
I. Resume, portfolio
II. Interview skills
III. Salary negotiation techniques
IV. A support system
        a.) Network
        b.) Recruiters
        c.) Temp agencies
        d.) Job/Career Services Centers
        e.) Online resources

A Mired Process

Supported by an ever growing, increasingly invasive
internet, the shrinking world of work has steadily
become employer dominant.
Corporations, government and other institutions
that hire continue to implement hindrances,
hurdles and hoops for job seekers whose desire is
to find employment that allows them a fair salary.
They seek an opportunity to apply their talent,
knowledge and skills in an environment that is
 respectful and appreciative of their contributions.
At a time in history when both actions and
decisions are one push of a button away, applicants
in search of employment are bewildered and
stressed by long waiting times and an interview
process that destroys hope, is costly and time wasting.
Are employers really seeking the best candidate?
Here is a key question Job Seekers deliberate:
Why does the job search process take so long?
So far, I have had 3, 4, 5, 7 interviews and am
still waiting…

Hope begins to wane after the first 3 interviews and this is understandable. Following are a list of suggestions that may help to boost your energy:

1. Continue to search and interview with other companies.
2. Remain fully engaged in your job search
3. Stay Positive... This may be hard but well worth the wait
4. Don't give in and settle for the first 'offer'
5. Realize that if one or two companies keep calling on you they most likely have a genuine interest in your skillset.
6. Continue to learn about the company and keep yourself motivated
7. Give them some options:
    A. Offer to work as a consultant
    B. Be open to partnering on special projects or assignments
    C. Ask if there is anything that you can do to speed up the decision making process... without appearing pushy.
8. Be ready to negotiate when the offer comes.

Limerick – 14

I Blew It!

I did not answer the initial call
And my reply was not polite at all
This time I admit
That I may have blown it
From the recruiter I got no recall.

Limerick – 15

No Certificate

Time ran out on my certificate
So much work to do I did forget
Despite a college degree
Outside the fence they put me
No more work 'til certificate update.

Limerick – 16

No Time To Read?

Employers today are a strange breed
When seeking new talent they need
Submit many say
A one page résumé
We simply don't have the time to read.

Limerick – 17

The Job Hopper

There was a well-trained job hopper
Who thought the old skills would keep her
She came to work late
After being out on a date
And the boss he kept her no longer.

Limerick – 18

Too Quiet

The interviewer a spirited soul
Met an applicant quiet as a mole
Some questions were raised
Answers were a gaze
So jobseeker went back to the hole.

Limerick – 19

Education

Although blessed with an education
There's still so much I don't understand
Years of schooling were great
Chased fate, even met my mate
Yet I can't compile a success plan.

Limerick – 20

Fair Pay

Though considered an educated mind
Per my success plan I am far behind
College educated
Academics berated
Fair paying jobs seem hardest to find.

Life Is Not All About Work

CHAPTER 5

Get Out, Get it, Grow!

Overview

Desire for success is natural for most if not all human beings. Without prior preparation however, many fall short or encounter hurdles that slow and sometimes dissuade progress.

It is my hope that the stories and poems in this chapter will challenge you to persevere in pursuit of your professional goals. Read on...

Possibilities Beckon

Possibilities are everywhere
Facing everyone who dares
To take on a new challenge
Hazard a beckoning opportunity
A risk?
Maybe!
But without that step you may never see
That everywhere there's possibility.

Lend a hand

Someone received help today
Who had the drive
But was oh so scared
Of that first step to be made

With the offer from an outstretched hand
And come on let's do this a wordless command
Courage was quickly gained
And a life-lasting leap was made.

Life Goes On!

Life is built in stages
No matter how you plan
Life comes and goes in stages
Dwell not on ageism
That merely is society's ploy
To distort one's progressive role

Life is built in stages
So actions you must take
Life will progress in stages
Irrespective of all that's at stake
To hold back limits one's potential
Sets the stage for a death spiral

Life is built in stages
Set goals or let it flow
Life is built in stages
And one must give and take
There is no way to prevent change
It's nature's plan well laid

Life is built in stages
And so adapt we must
Life will progress in stages
Open your mind lest it turns to dust
What happens next no one can predict
Matters not which stage you're at

Because life is built in stages
A progress plan to write
Strive for riches
Build only bridges
Allow freedom always to flow

Because life is built in stages
For knowledge, food and shelter
No human being should starve
Each individual has unique value
Everyone their path must carve

So step aside at times
Allow momentum to flow
Life goes by in stages
Progressive minds all know
For someone else to take the lead
Continuum must be built
So help others to come on board
As farewell draws near its close
To step off life's stage will be a thrill
And gracefully you are sure to go.

Position Yourself

In a new position
Position yourself
Learn all that you can
Attain mastery
In the shortest time
Become the resource
And when you've outgrown that place
Move on to a new more challenging space.

A Painful Conversation

Are you looking for a job?
Yes! I need a job!
What makes you so sure
That a job is what you need?
What do you mean?
They closed the position I had
And I need money…
Bills! I've got bills to pay, and job or no job
Caesar wants his money – every month…
Do you still live at your parent's' house?
So what? Does that mean I don't have bills?
You don't know me
Yes I do!
You are young,
You are educated beyond your years
You are gifted
With as much talent as anyone in your field
You don't need a job!
Okay! Since you know so much
What do I need?
I am hungry, I am broke and…Tears flow
Pause…
I have no life right now
Since graduation, everything is a struggle
What was the point?…. *Pause*
All my friends, everyone I know has more money
They always seem to be having fun

They travel and live comfortably
But here I am almost thirty
With my 'degrees'
Struggling, living at home!
What ever happened to:
"Go to college, get an education"
You will earn more,
Have a higher standard of living?
Really! Just a load of BS.
My friends barely have a certificate
But, look at my parents, look at me
and the rest of us with our 'degrees'
No job… or none that pays a fair salary
All these years later we're still in debt!
Everything that you say is true, however
The world has changed
And the recession didn't help anyone
But you must be patient
A door will open
I want to believe you
But in the meantime
Should I just starve?
Or, just settle for whatever?
How long? Since you've been here before
How long do I have to endure this degrading life?

Have you thought of building a career?
Yes! I heard that before
But how am I to build a career
If I can't even get a job
Much less get my foot in the door?
Two years ago when I lost my first job
We had this career conversation
What am I doing wrong?
I have the qualifications
I am as good as, if not better than
everyone in the department
What is wrong with me?... *Tears flow*
Pause...
Building a career takes time
And now that you have some experience
to support your qualification
You have to plan
What you want to do
Where you want to work
How much you want to earn
Even the rank you want
Your office appearance and location
Must be part of your plan
Visualize it, close your eyes...
Can you see what you are wearing?

Picture yourself walking in on day one
Then you work towards it...Focus!
Think career!
Jobs are merely a quick fix
They are easy to get
Never last very long and
Were never meant to make you rich
A career on the other hand
Takes time to build...and must be nurtured
Thus, a career is more gratifying
Careers last longer –
Perhaps even a lifetime if you choose
A career is more financially rewarding over time
Because this is your specialty
Your passion
As you progress, experience counts
Exposure leads to inclusion
and advancement;
Building a career demands focus
It demands commitment;
Continuing education as you progress
will bring you everlasting respect
and recognition.
So! Those are your choices
Time to make a decision
Do you want a job or
Will you apply the knowledge and skills that you
earned to build your career?

Pillars of Success

Build from foundation to the sky
Stand by core values and beliefs
Achieve without sacrificing self-worth
Grow from desire to success
Walk with dignity and pride
Speak intelligently and factually
Listen with sincerity and focus

KNOW YOUR HISTORY, REINFORCE FUNDAMENTALS

V	C	C	R	P
I	O	O	E	E
S	M	N	A	R
I	P	V	L	S
O	E	I	I	E
N	T	C	S	V
	E	T	T	E
	N	I	I	R
	C	O	C	E
	E	N		

Get Paid

The salary was never meant
to make any employee rich.
If riches are what you desire,
Become an entrepreneur
A creator, an innovator
Be the voice behind the decision
and cash in on the outcome.

Overcome Obstacles

Life is filled with twists and turns
Obstacles wait everywhere
From the jobs you do to the friends you earn
They linger somewhere out there;
When you encounter hindrances
Acknowledge and let them pass
Choose well and do the things you should
To progress in your class.

Help for the Helper

Day after day for weeks it seemed
My value, my worth I doubted
Most cherished are the daily duties
And the lives I've touched
Those nagging questions, not so much…
Why do I do this, why do I take this drive?
Why do I endure this hassle?
With motivation waning -
Life's burdens and bureaucracy dragging me down
Upliftment for my now weakened spirit was sought
And, to a mature client I vented
In a few simple words, direct and without froth
An experienced response came forth:
The job that you do, is not about you
Think only of those that you serve!
Let not work, hassle, and the drive that you endure
Be the cause to retract from your call…
This is your purpose and you do it well
Think only of those that you serve!
It took but an instant for this simple message
To reignite and restore my passion
The doubt that had grown, in an instant was gone
It took a different perspective,
But one well worth hearing
And my drive to serve others goes on.

Be Free

Turn off the noise and distractions
Open your mind to new exploration
Test new horizons
And note your own ideas
As they burst out with explosive force.

Muster the courage to challenge yourself
Let not your talent be wasted
Nor mental obstacles shelve
Greatness lives inside
Unleash your gifts, watch them float worldwide.

Unclench your palms, unplug your ears
Be free to grasp knowledge missed in past years
Fearless persistent force
Listening, growing, wanting more
Let nature take its course.

Change

Sometimes in our effort to avoid change
Life throws us little curves
Compelling us to rethink our perspective...
Examine our decisions,
Alter our course of actions.

Sometimes we are forced from our traditional ways
Because of a greater plan yet to be unveiled
To divert from that one track we've been on
In preparation for new knowledge - new direction.

Sometimes one must leave that well-worn path
See different places, different faces
Nothing memory can trace
Allow the freshness of unfamiliar to exhilarate
Open, feel as your heart beat increases its pace.

Sometimes as each new challenge beckons
An innate hunger for adventure gradually responds
Now eager, without thought you chase the lure
Change has come
And this enriched life means so much more.

Limiting Perceptions

Human beings upon self-reflection often realize that they are bound by self-imposed limitations, more-so than perceived institutional barriers.

Success Mission

Success is more easily attained when core values and beliefs remain central throughout the mission.

Small Steps

                                    and take action.
                          question
                    observe,
              to touch,
Allow your innate curiosity

Open

Many are hindered from progress by their own limiting beliefs which once overcome, often leads to great strides, more open doors and new opportunities.

A Test of Will

Watch as the tide flows back and forth
Allow time to learn
Memorize each ebb and flow
Make mental note of every pattern
Calculate, internally process
Look closely at the flotsam
Shape, size, girth, rugged or smooth
Will any bear your weight?
Support may be needed in the straights
Figure out how to avoid the debris
Collect only edible matter
And after much calculation
With cautious aggression
Make your entry as the tide recedes
Ride the wave, float over the calm
Avoid swells and any signs of turbulence
Focus at all cost must be maintained
Confidence must intact remain...
And as the tide turns
Take control
Be propelled by physical gifts
Applying consistent motion to stay the course
Persist amidst the pain
Overcome the stressors
Until the horizon gives way to final destination
Resist the urge to rest

Draw on superior physical and mental capacities
Exercise control, patience
No need for a final surge
And upon arrival
Immediately begin conditioning for the next crossing
A seemingly endless sequence of horizons
Constantly evolving
Each with its own channels,
Unique challenges
Life's journey is merely a test of will
Waiting to be conquered.

Limerick – 21

Desire Beats Barrier

My father at sixty four retired
Bought a gadget with which he flirted
Nights he barely slept
Daily his eyes wept
Until that computer he mastered.

Life Is Not All About Work

CHAPTER 6

Embrace Experience

Overview

Stories are continually told about the disrespect and subsequent dismissal faced by many experienced employees. These acts of attrition may be based on one, or multiple factors. Employees at any or every stage of their careers however, need to keep abreast of trends in employment and continually upgrade their skills. Additionally, 'retirement' needs to be factored into everyone's career plan.

No one's life or lifestyle should be all about work. Likewise, working until death should never be a must. If life seems to be leaning in that direction, NOW is the time to make some adjustments. Be motivated. Invest time and effort in activities other than 'work'. Read on...

Time Flies

All my life I heard time flies
And until now didn't understand why
I must have been too young to realize
Time flies by like birds in the sky.

Time passes quickly when one's busy
I heard my elders say
So I found a job, worked hard everyday
Until now I am old and grey.

Time goes faster as we get older
I heard that story too
And now I'm stuck with two
First I worked hard and now am old
And oh, what can I do?

But I was honest and helped some folks
Who took some time to explore the world
Their stories told of all I missed
And the joys that traveling offered.

Full life yes, regrets some too
But reflecting now as time flies by
Each day brings something new
And my life of helping others
Is an everlasting attribute.

Lifespan

Teens and twenties
Are a life of fun
The whole world to explore
Energetic, with youthful hormones bubbling
These know-it-alls, their illusion will outgrow.
In the thirties
Now position yourself
Time for family, hard work, and more
Test your value, seek professional growth
Reinforce your knowledge and worth.
The forties
May be a testing time
Teenage children's needs to meet
Now challenges rapidly multiply
Life's demands just won't be beat.
In the fifties
Experience sells
Grandchildren are growing fast
For all those who care, the educator you are
Saving history from being lost.
In the sixties
Condition for retirement
Before you are too old to care
Spend time with family and friends
Live large and without fear.
The seventies
Watch the youngsters take charge
Share stories of a life well known
And although from here on your pace may slow
Command respect,
Volumes your wisdom speaks
Cherish each moment as they arise.

Progress!?

Imagine:
A world where no one had to go to work,
But, everyone had enough to eat,
Time to rest, time for family
Life was outdoors, echoed with laughter, frolicking; fun.

Imagine:
A time when only the men went out to work
The women stayed home
Caring for the men and children was their role
There was enough to eat
Families enjoyed dinner together
Story time took place before bedtime
During this time, families were closer
Divorces were few - shameful if they became final
And children were secure,
well-mannered and respectful.

Imagine:
A world where men and women go to work
Grandparents living in elderly care facilities get visitors
Relegated to childminders and disciplinarians
are the teachers
Television keeps latchkey kids off the street
As parents struggle to make ends meet.

Imagine:
A world in which everyone must work
Four generations share the workplace burden
A never before seen phenomenon
Some say it's change for the better, others not so sure
For most working class households are as good as poor.

Now ask yourself:
How did we get here?
Was it laziness, poor planning, lack of education?
Does stupidity or government oversight play a part?
Is it lack of commonsense, disrespect for humanity?

It's sad:
Commonsense is not at all common
Because if it were, perhaps the benefits of equality
Would inspire unity among the working class
And corporate dominance driven by capitalist greed
Supported by elected government ineptitude
Would fail!

Life, Passion and Exploitation

Where's the joy in following my passion
Giving time and talent to some greedy establishment
Whose moronic goal is to tap all that I have learned
and labored to achieve
To further bulge insatiable coffers
For a mere pittance in remittance;
Meanwhile their corporation expands into trillions
Fame carries the name to new talent
Who too will wander into their trap of exploitation;
No more!
It took a while for reality to hit home
Another lesson learned;
Now my passion is reserved for businesses
Beneficial only to me, my partners, my friends and family
And those that care enough to invest in me financially;
Life is not all about work
Life is not all about play
Life is not all about going after your passion
Or chasing some lucid dream
Life is not all about raising children
Learning, or slaving for the highest bidder
Life is neither one thing nor the other
This template keeps changing form
No matter where you're from
Life's twists and turns go on
And with the promise of simplicity
Is as complex as can be
Chasing passion, raising children
Following after your dreams
Are the stages of life, and variations of fun
That a life well lived truly is.

No Regrets

I miss the folks I worked alongside
Somedays I miss the routine
Those client conversations
Visions of horizons unforeseen

The office gossip amused sometimes
'Though most times they were mundane
Now I walk away without remorse
To challenge the untested brain

With bureaucracy and routine now behind
Life decisions are all about me
Day and night my time is mine
To become all that I can be.

Joyous Moment

This person over 60
Had worked every day since 20
It's what I do, it's all I know
A story told countless times before
Then came the day of letting go
And tears of joy did flow
I know not what is there to do
Nor when, nor where, nor how
With time all mine… I can think now
No need to rush, no deadline to meet
Believe me, I need no plan
In time, I'll figure it out.

Forgotten Values

While I was busy working
My family grew apart
First my spouse
Then our house
And our offspring followed fast.

While I was busy working
My personal health declined
From constant toil and diet foiled
By poor meals and little time to recline.

While I was busy working
It was noted that I'd changed...
Forgotten now the person I was
All that mattered were the dollars.

Momentarily one day I paused
To take a glance backwards
Very quickly it was realized
That while I was busy working
My standards had been devalued.

Liberation

Thoughts of going back to work today
Upset me really bad
This vacation presented another choice
To leave the fun I've had now is hard
Confirming work is not my only vice

Don't get me wrong, I'm excellent
Joyful is the work I do
But long gone are the demands for rent
So with no agenda, to me I'm true
Liberation is the sand between my toes

In reflection I briefly ponder
For forty years I gave it all
Fully invested, work was my priority
Today my life comes first, not walls
No dependents now – my family is all grown

Standing on this sunlit beach
The world is there to see
No rush hour hustle, home's easy to reach
With commuting no longer a worry
I desire open country and adventure

Now living in this moment
In my heart I feel secure
No deadlines morning or evening
As I watch, the seagulls soar
And the sunset before snoring

When the day dawned, I did fulfill
One final business courtesy
I made a call, bid the job farewell
Before the sun rose above fruit trees
No more commitment to work, I'm free.

Busier than Ever!

"Retirement is a fulltime job!"
That's what my father said
"I'm busier now than I have ever been"
Is what my father said!

There's a world out there to see
And oh gosh, I'm so busy
Catching up with the past…
Time is moving so fast
Come ride along with me.

So much to see, so much to do
Finding a break is not easy
Another trip to plan
For this journey I'm on
This lifestyle is living the dream

Sleep and eat wherever I land
Nature now calls more often
Frequent rest stops the body demands
While the clock ticks down, and on.

CHAPTER 7

It's All About Me

Overview

When all is said and done, your career choice and the decisions that follow need to be entirely about you, your goals, your aspirations. In reviewing the following self-examinations, be honest with your responses. Then, use your discovery as a guide, or call to action that which will help in equipping you for your next move. Be successful! Read on...

Peace of Mind

Having peace of mind in your workplace is one way to get half of the job done. Which of the following time tested tips do you practice? (Y = Yes, N = No)

Y / N I surround myself with art, language, music, quotes etc. with positive, empowering and inspiring. messages

Y / N I interact with colleagues who challenge me to grow personally and professionally

Y / N I collaborate with individuals and groups that motivate and inspire me through positive thoughts, and actions

Y / N I laugh often and contribute to tasteful humor

Y / N I am well positioned and am on a pathway to professional growth in my industry

Y / N I am constantly examining new opportunities and exploring next steps

Y / N I demonstrate a positive attitude irrespective of the situation or demand

Y / N I continually seek opportunities to learn, build my skills and share my knowledge

Y / N My day begins with a prayer, meditation or other activity that helps me to relax

Y / N I get to work early enough to unwind from the journey

Y / N My to-do list is habitually done either the day before or first thing at the start of my shift

Y / N I have a mentor… who is not a spouse, immediate family member or close friend

Y / N   I walk away from the desk at least once each hour to ease my mind and rest my eyes

Y / N   Fresh air is a great energizer for me so I take mini breaks to walk outside all year round

Y / N   I stretch my limbs continually to relieve tension and improve blood circulation

Y / N   I always ask for clarification to ensure that directives related to my duties are clear

Y / N   I document my actions and interactions daily, especially those with superiors

Y / N   I give respect and appreciation to everyone who supports my role

Y / N   I monitor trends in my industry and keep my resume updated

Y / N   I demonstrate confidence in my knowledge and in communication with everyone

Y / N   I make it my business to know the policies and procedures of my workplace

Y / N   I manage my time effectively

Y / N   I have friends and/or close acquaintances who are not colleagues or co-workers

Y / N   I support my co-workers

Y / N   I contribute to the fulfillment of the department's mission

Y / N   I present myself appropriately for the task at hand

Y / N   I am focused when in my work zone

In Another Life

Complete each statement beginning 'I would' to express three things you would seek to accomplish in each of the four areas below.

If I had the time:

I would…

I would

I would

If I didn't have children:

I would

I would

I would

If I had extra money:

I would

I would

I would

If I didn't have to work:

I would

I would

I would

Now that you have decided what your alternate life would be, perhaps it is time to draft a plan to make it happen.

Finding Balance

Complete the following statements by circling the word or phrase in parenthesis that matches your experience.

What I like most about my job is…(*It's my hobby, It pays well, I schedule my hours, I pace myself*)

In my job I least enjoy… (*My co-workers, the hours, the cleanup, the routine, the job*)

My work environment is… (*Toxic, clean, pleasant, boring, exciting*)

Outside of work I…

Currently I work ___ job(s)

I have none-work related activities (*Yes, No, sometimes, weekly, monthly, daily, never*)

When not at work I am… (*Sleeping, with family, doing chores, exercising, hanging out, gardening*)

I have no desire to take time off work… (*True, False*)

I have no vacation available… (*True, False, I never take vacation, vacation time is for childcare*)

It is easier for me to get work done at home… (*Yes, No, I never take work home, sometimes*)

When I leave the job I leave the work behind… (*Yes, No, sometimes, except for special projects*)

My friends say I am always working… (*True, False, I just don't want to be bothered*)

The money doesn't matter to me if I enjoy my work… (*True, False*)

Long commutes are… (*Tiring, excellent, not good, time wasting, an obstacle, okay*)

My co-workers are the only friends I have (*True, False*)

My job is my hobby (*True, False*)

Life Lines

The commonly used exclamations below are lines often used by individuals to express their state of affairs when they encounter challenges or successes.

Choose **one** definition of the life Lines that best characterizes your life or lifestyle.

1. Life is too short.

2. While life lasts…

3. Life goes on.

4. Life is not without trials.

5. Life has its ups and downs.

6. Life is great/wonderful.

7. Life couldn't be better.

8. My life is a living hell.

9. In all my life, I have never….

10. Life is too hard.

11. Life sucks!

12. Oh life!

13. What a life?

Why have you chosen number_____?

Is it supporting or dragging you down?

What actions must you take to change your view in order to alter this situation?

Complete the statement below that will confirm your decision to change/improve the path your life or career is on:

In order to improve the quality of life for my family (and or) myself I must _____.

Finding Balance 2

Y / N   I get to work on time with sufficient time to unwind before starting my day.

Y / N   I drive ten miles or less to work.

Y / N   My 10 mile drive usually takes over an hour.

Y / N   I have a stressful workload.

Y / N   My work environment is toxic and causes stress.

Y / N   My workplace could use sanitizing and a facelift.

Y / N   I frequently cover for others but no one does for me.

Y / N   I always leave work on time.

Y / N   I am too tired after work to enjoy family time.

Y / N   After work I am energetic and able to enjoy time with family and friends.

Y / N   My salary affords me flexible spending.

Y / N   In order to keep up with my responsibilities, I must take work home.

Y / N   I take breaks at work.

Y / N   My job allows me the flexibility to take breaks.

Y / N   I am able to interact with coworkers without feeling pressured or stressed.

continued on the following page

Y / N   My manager/supervisor and I are partners in decisions directly related to my role.

Y / N   On days off, I am often asked to come to work or to answer questions about work.

Y / N   I do not worry about work when on vacation.

Y / N   I use public transportation.

Y / N   I currently work in my chosen career.

Y / N   In order to make ends meet I must work two jobs.

Y / N   My salary aligns with my qualifications.

Y / N   I am allowed to take breaks at work.

Keyword Index

A
Attitude, Advised, Arrived, Appreciation
Accounts, Academics, Action

B
Bookkeeping, Bills, Building, Burnout
Barriers, Business, Best, Bright

C
Career, Culture, Certificate, Clarity
College, Commuters, Capitalism
Choose, Confident, Competent
Caring, Committed, Class, Customers
Corporations, Communication, Colors

D
Drive, Debated, Dinner, Diet
Discrimination, Dreams, Decision

E
Employer, Education, Energy, Empowered
Emotion, Employees, Enthusiasm, E-mail
Environment, Employment, Earth, Ethnic

F
Facts, Friends, Fun, Food
Focus, Family, Free

G
Gratitude, God, Gym, Government
Goals, Grow, Graduation

H
Health, Humor, Hiring, Helpful
Humble, Honest, Hope, Heart, Human

I
Intelligent, Inspiration, Interview
Idea, Impact, Income, Integrity
Industries, Interviewing

J
Job search

K
Knowledgeable, Kind

L
Learn, Listen, Language, Loyalty
Leaders, Looks, Life, Laugh

M
Motivation, Music, Managers
Military, Mentor, Memory
Motivate, Market, Money

N
Nurturing, Network

O
Organized, Online, Open
Open-minded, Outcome

P

Productive, Persistent, Participate,
People, Partnership, Position, Prayer
Priorities, Politician, Plan, Present
Politeness, Paid, Politics, Peace,

Q

Qualified, Quantity, Quality

R

Retirement, Respectful, Relax, Rewarded
Routine, Rise, Rules, Risk, Retire
Relevant, Recruiters, Research

S

Supportive, Student, Smile, Supervisor
Serve, Sacrifice, success, Stress,
Skills, Salary, Successful, Spend, Seek, Sincere

T

Teamwork, Talent, Team, Time
Travel, Training, Television, Train

U

Unity

V

Value, Values, Vision, Visionary
Veteran, Volunteer

W

Work, Wisdom

Key Phrases

At will

Career decision making

Career services centers

Caring and politeness

Core values

Educate, train and motivate

Employer benefits

Energy and drive

Family life

Hiring manager

Institutional barriers

Jobs well done

Less productivity

Life balance

Management notices

Messages of hope

Motivate others

Movers and shakers

Office gossip

Office politics

Open-mind

Peace of mind

Personal health

Place of service

Positive outlook

Relaxed environment

Seek employment

Self-examinations

Self-reflection

Service is delivered

Social media forums

Social services

Work-life balance

Workplace must be fun

About the Author

Carl Edgecombe holds a Master's Degree in Vocational and Technical Education from the State University of New York. Following his graduation in 1999, he spent a year abroad - first in his volcano devastated homeland of Montserrat where he was asked to fill the position of Music Teacher.

Later that year he had a brief stint working as a Support Specialist, serving students with special needs in Essex, England. Upon returning to the United States, he entered the world of College Residence Life where he discovered his passion for the field of Career Services.

More than ten years later, he has matured into a respected Master Career Specialist and Workforce Development Practitioner. He has utilized his knowledge as a Global Career Development Facilitator; Licensed Federal Résumé Writer and Career Coach to educate and train populations in various arenas of Higher Education and American Job Centers.

(continued on the following page)

(continued from the previous page)

Carl has created and hosted presentations such as: 'Be Who You Are', and 'Re-Educate, Retire and Re-Invent Yourself' On the national level, he has blogged on career-related issues as well as co-wrote and facilitated: 'Reaching the Dream of Social Justice: Using Narrative, Systems, and Solution Focused Interventions in Career' (2009) 'Strategies for Providing Career Guidance to Students of Diverse Cultural Ethnic and International Backgrounds' (2011) at National Career Development Association (NCDA) conferences. Carl is making his debut as an author, publishing this book *Life Is Not All About Work*.

If you have any questions or comments for the author, he may be reached at careerchoiceblog@gmail.com.